Weekly iron and folic acid supplementation programmes for women of reproductive age

An analysis of best programme practices

SHORT VERSION

WHO Library Cataloguing in Publication Data

Weekly iron and folic acid supplementation programmes for women of reproductive age: an analysis of best programme practices (short version)

1. Anaemia, Iron-Deficiency–prevention and control. 2. Iron. 3. Folic acid. 4. Dietary supplements. 5. Women's health.

ISBN 978 92 9061 524 8   (NLM Classification: WA 309)

© World Health Organization 2011

All rights reserved. Publications of the World Health Organization can be obtained from WHO Press, World Health Organization, 20 Avenue Appia, 1211 Geneva 27, Switzerland (tel.: +41 22 791 3264; fax: +41 22 791 4857; e-mail: bookorders@who.int). Requests for permission to reproduce or translate WHO publications – whether for sale or for noncommercial distribution – should be addressed to WHO Press, at the above address (fax: +41 22 791 4806; e-mail: permissions@who.int). For WHO Western Pacific Regional Publications, request for permission to reproduce should be addressed to the Publications Office, World Health Organization, Regional Office for the Western Pacific, P.O. Box 2932, 1000, Manila, Philippines, (fax: +632 521 1036, e-mail: publications@wpro.who.int).

The designations employed and the presentation of the material in this publication do not imply the expression of any opinion whatsoever on the part of the World Health Organization concerning the legal status of any country, territory, city or area or of its authorities, or concerning the delimitation of its frontiers or boundaries. Dotted lines on maps represent approximate border lines for which there may not yet be full agreement.

The mention of specific companies or of certain manufacturers' products does not imply that they are endorsed or recommended by the World Health Organization in preference to others of a similar nature that are not mentioned. Errors and omissions excepted, the names of proprietary products are distinguished by initial capital letters.

All reasonable precautions have been taken by the World Health Organization to verify the information contained in this publication. However, the published material is being distributed without warranty of any kind, either expressed or implied. The responsibility for the interpretation and use of the material lies with the reader. In no event shall the World Health Organization be liable for damages arising from its use.

Table of Contents

Executive summary	1
What is the issue?	1
How was information gathered?	2
What strategies were effective in supporting women to take WIFS?	3
What information does this study contain?	4
Best programme practices	5
1. Assessing iron deficiency and anaemia problems	5
2. Revisiting the anaemia control programme strategies in countries	6
3. Advocacy and formulation of policy	7
4. Target population and strategy for accessing IFA supplements	10
5. Composition, presentation and supply of IFA supplements	12
6. Procurement and delivery of IFA supplements	15
7. Communication strategy to create demand and improve coverage and compliance	18
8. Capacity development	24
9. Monitoring	27
10. Evaluation	28
BEST PRACTICE TOP 10	30

Executive summary

What is the issue?

> One out of three WRA is estimated to be anaemic. Non-pregnant women are the population group with the greatest number of individuals affected by anaemia (468.4 million).

In a developing country, provision of weekly iron and folic acid supplements (WIFS) to women of reproductive age (WRA) should be viewed as one of the most important nutrition interventions. Globally, 1.62 billion people are anaemic, many due to iron deficiency[1]. One out of three WRA is estimated to be anaemic[2]. Non-pregnant women are the population group with the greatest number of individuals affected by anaemia (468.4 million)[1]. The consequences of iron deficiency, particularly for WRA, are far-reaching. Iron deficiency contributes to maternal mortality, foetal growth retardation and perinatal mortality. Research has shown that improving iron and folate nutrition, not only influences safe motherhood and birth outcomes, but also enhances the health and well-being of WRA by optimizing educational performance and increasing overall productivity.

Unfortunately, past approaches have not been effective in preventing and controlling iron deficiency and anaemia. The WHO Global Consultation on Weekly Iron and Folic Acid Supplementation for Preventing Anaemia in Women of Reproductive Age (April 2007) therefore reached the consensus that critical elements of WIFS programmes must be identified to ensure the successful implementation of such programmes worldwide and, ultimately, to improve the iron status of WRA and reduce the prevalence of anaemia[2]. A study was therefore undertaken in 2008–2009 with the objective of identifying best programme practices for planning and implementation of WIFS programmes.

---

1   *World prevalence of anaemia 1993-2005.,* World Health Organization, Geneva, 2008.

2   McLean E, *et al.* Worldwide prevalence of anaemia in preschool aged children, pregnant women and non-pregnant women of reproductive age In: Kraemer K, Zimmermann MB, eds. *Nutritional anemia.* Sight and Life Press, 2007.

It is envisaged that the information on critical programme elements and practices drawn together in this document will serve as a guideline to support advocacy, accelerate planning and strengthen implementation of WIFS programmes for WRA by programme planners and managers.

How was information gathered?

The first step of the study involved defining the criteria for selection of WIFS programmes for WRA. Based on agreed criteria, 10 programmes were identified. A standard template was used to gather programme information and document case studies. These case studies were analysed in terms of:

- strategy;
- intervention package and implementation process;
- critical programme components, including type of iron-folic acid (IFA) supplements used, logistics management and distribution channel;
- innovative, effective actions for improving compliance; and
- monitoring mechanisms.

Lessons learnt were summarised and best programme practices were extracted.

A major constraint in the study was the fact that the process documentation of the programmes was often incomplete. This resulted in intensive follow-up with implementers to fill in the gaps, and made the documentation of case studies a complex exercise.

A total of 10 programmes across six countries were identified: two from Viet Nam, four from India and the remaining four from Cambodia, Egypt, the Lao People's Democratic Republic and the Philippines. In all the programmes, except one in Viet Nam, the target population included adolescent girls both in and out of school. The WIFS programme in Egypt was the only one to include both adolescent boys and girls.

Two distinct programme processes were used:

1. Free supply of WIFS to WRA, accompanied by nutrition education.
2. Selling of iron-folic acid (IFA) supplements to WRA using a social marketing approach.

Two distinct programme processes were used:

1. free supply of WIFS to WRA, accompanied by nutrition education; and
2. selling of IFA supplements to WRA using a social-marketing approach.

Seven programmes utilized the first process, with Cambodia, the Philippines and Hai Duong Province in Viet Nam using the second strategy. Interestingly, the Lao People's Democratic Republic used a social-marketing approach to create demand, but supplied WIFS to WRA free of cost. Six of the ten programmes were scaled to include the entire region, four of those providing IFA free of cost.

WIFS tablets used across the programmes varied in composition. Elemental iron content was either 60 mg or 100 mg, while folic acid content ranged from 0.3 mg to 3.5 mg. No rationale was presented regarding the selection of composition for the supplement. Cost varied from US$0.12 to US$3.64 for an annual supply of 52 IFA supplements. The delivery channels for WIFS were not limited to the health sector, but also included schools, institutions, factories, women's groups, etc. Biannual administration of deworming was undertaken in six of the 10 programmes. In a period of 6-16 months, there was a wide difference in the reductions in anaemia prevalence, ranging from 8.9% to 56.8%. The cost of the programme per WRA / year varied from US $0.15 to US$ 5.00 / day, the highest cost being observed in programmes using an intensive social marketing approach. WIFS compliance was almost 70% or above in all WIFS programmes except one.

What strategies were effective in supporting women to take WIFS?

The practice of fixing one day in the week as "WIFS Day" or "Iron Day" to promote WIFS consumption was universal. Such a strategy addressed the problem of "forgetfulness", a primary factor adversely influencing compliance. Adverse side-effects of WIFS were rather low, between 5% to 20%, and therefore had little impact on compliance. Promoting the consumption of IFA on a full stomach before retiring at night further contributed to addressing the issue of adverse side-effects. A communication strategy emphasizing the benefits of WIFS experienced by WRA, rather than adverse side-effects, played a positive role in creating demand for WIFS and increasing compliance. Health and nutrition education and social-marketing strategies, often based on formative research, along with advocacy and social mobilization activities, improved acceptance of iron supplementation. Establishing a simple, user-friendly monitoring system played a critical role in modifying programme design and sustaining the improved compliance rate. Individual self-monitoring or institution-based monitoring was considered practical, feasible and effective. Investing in supervision during WIFS consumption was not feasible and provided no added value compared with monitoring.

What information does this study contain?

The study presents the case studies of 10 WIFS programmes in six countries, and reviews the WIFS practices emerging from analysis of the programmes reviewed, highlighting details of best programme practices with reference to target population and strategy for accessing IFA supplements. It also provides information on delivery mechanisms for IFA supplements, critical elements of communication strategies, actions for improving compliance, user-friendly monitoring systems and the principles followed for capacity development.

> What solutions does this study propose?
>
> This study proposes the use of a two-pronged approach in developing countries for improvement of iron nutrition and prevention of iron deficiency anaemia:
>
> - free WIFS supply accompanied by nutrition education for socioeconomically disadvantaged groups; and
>
> - investment in social marketing of WIFS to WRA who have the resources to purchase low-cost IFA supplements.

For the full version of the Best Practices Study, please see the document, *Weekly iron and folic acid supplementation programmes for women of reproductive age: an analysis of best programme practices*. Manila, World Health Organization Regional Office for the Western Pacific, 2011. Both the short and full version can be found on the WHO WPRO website at: http://www.wpro.who.int/health_topics/nutrition/publications.htm

Best programme practices

A total of 10 large-scale WIFS programmes for WRA were analysed to synthesize the best programme strategy and activities for improving iron and folate status and reducing anaemia prevalence in WRA. The information presented is intended to serve as a planning and implementation guide for policy-makers, programme managers and planners of WIFS programmes.

1. Assessing iron deficiency and anaemia problems

> It is essential to create a database on the prevalence of anaemia and ID in WRA prior to considering the introduction of WIFS as a public health measure in a region. Information on causative factors of ID is important in deciding on the most effective action needed to improve the iron-nutrition status of WRA.

It is well documented that ID is the single most common cause of anaemia in pregnant women as well as the WRA group, which includes adolescent girls 10-19 years who have attained menarche. According to international criteria, iron deficiency (ID) and iron deficiency anemia (IDA) is a severe public health problem in a region when the prevalence of anaemia in pregnant women is over 40%. It is a moderate public health problem if the anaemia prevalence is between 20-39% . Haemoglobin cut-off values for defining anaemia in various population groups are presented in Table 1 and are useful for assessing anaemia prevalence. Once IDA is established as a public health problem, building pre-pregnancy iron stores and preventing anaemia in WRA is essential. Surveys and secondary information need to be reviewed in order to understand the factors contributing to ID and to work out an implementation plan package for a WIFS programme for WRA.

It is well documented that ID is the single most common cause of anaemia in pregnant women as well as the WRA group, which includes adolescent girls 10-19 years who have attained menarche. According to international criteria, iron deficiency (ID) and iron deficiency anemia (IDA) is a severe public health problem in a region when the prevalence of anaemia in pregnant women is over 40%. It is a moderate public health problem if the anaemia prevalence is between 20–39%[3]. Haemoglobin cut-off values for defining anaemia in various population groups are presented in Table 1 and are useful for assessing anaemia prevalence. Once IDA is established as a public health problem, building pre-pregnancy iron stores and preventing anaemia in WRA is essential. Surveys and secondary information need to be reviewed in order to understand the factors contributing to ID and to work out an implementation plan package for a WIFS programme for WRA.

Table 1: Haemoglobin and haematocrit cut-offs used to define anaemia in people living at sea level		
Age or sex group	Haemoglobin level (g/dl)	Haematocrit below (%)
Children 6 months to 4 years	11.0	33
Children 5 -11 years	11.5	34
Children 12 -14 years	12.0	36
Non-pregnant women	12.0	36
Pregnant women	11.0	33
Men	13.0	39

Source: *Iron deficiency anaemia: assessment, prevention, and control. A guide for programme managers.* Geneva, World Health Organization, 2001 (WHO/NHD/01.3).

2. Revisiting the anaemia control programme strategies in countries

In order to place improvement of iron nutrition and reduction of anaemia high on the political agenda, advocacy needs to emphasize the economic and health benefits of WIFS for WRA and the cost-effectiveness of this intervention. Developing policies regarding the prevention of ID and anaemia in WRA is essential in securing resources and funding, establishing successful programme strategies and legitimizing and sustaining implementation of WIFS programmes. A high profile launch is useful in mobilizing political support.

---

3   Preventing ID in women and children: Technical consensus on key issues. A UNICEF/UNU/WHO/MI technical workshop, 7-9 October 1998.

The problem of ID and anaemia should be viewed, not only as a serious public health problem during pregnancy, but also as a serious health problem in WRA. Existing anaemia prevention and management policies therefore need to be reviewed to consider the inclusion of preventive measures such as WIFS for WRA in the public health policy of the country. Reviews of programmes reveal that WIFS is a practical strategy for preventing anaemia in non-pregnant WRA and results in a number of benefits, such as:

- reducing tiredness;
- improving energy levels and working capacity;
- improving learning ability and school performance;
- regularizing menstruation, improving iron store;
- enhancing skin glow, and
- building pre-pregnancy iron stores.

The recommendations of the WHO Global Consultation and WHO position statement on WIFS for WRA, combined with examples of successful WIFS case studies, could form the basis for national consultations towards revisiting the programme strategy for anaemia control. To formulate such a strategy, it is important that national consultations are not confined to the health and nutrition sectors of government, but involve wider participation, including representatives from: departments of education, women's development, rural development, youth development, mass communication, and sections of the private sector representatives that primarily have a female work force such as: garment factories, tea estates; pharmaceutical groups; advertising agencies; and social-marketing agencies.

3. Advocacy and formulation of policy

It is crucial to inform policy-makers of the serious implications of ID and anaemia for school performance, pregnancy outcome and productivity. The important economic losses to countries and families as a result of ID and the corresponding gains achieved by preventing such deficiency need to be appreciated. Equally important is the need to inform all involved of the benefits of WIFS and the effects of such interventions on MDG progress. Table 2 highlights the relationship between anaemia control in WRA and the MDGs. Such information supports WIFS programme advocacy and facilitates decisions by policy-makers and planners to include WIFS programmes as part of measures to improve the health of WRA and improve iron status.

Policy-makers need to be made aware of the low cost of WIFS interventions compared with the high cost of ID and anaemia for national health, productivity and the economy. Case studies from three large-scale programmes in India and Egypt indicate that the annual cost of WIFS programmes for adolescent girls can be as low as US$0.15 to US$0.36 per recipient. IFA supplements make up only about one third of that total cost. Moreover, cost-analysis data from the Uttar Pradesh WIFS programme reveal that the total project cost per WRA is reduced significantly when programmes are taken to scale and cover a larger number of WRA. Sharing such information with policy-makers will aid in securing resources to address the serious public health issues caused by ID and anaemia, particularly in adolescent girls and pre-pregnant women.

Table 2: ID and IDA prevention in WRA through WIFS helps to achieve the MDGs

MDG Goals	Impact of IDA Prevention
MDG # 1 Eradicate extreme poverty and hunger	• Increases the body's capacity to do work (for every 10% increase in HB – 15% increase in physical work). • Reduces low birth weight. • Reduces undernutrition in children under five years.
MDG # 2 Achieve universal primary education	• Reduces the frequency and severity of infections / morbidity and mortality. • Increases school attendance, retention, learning capacity and school achievement.
MDG # 3 Promote gender equality and empower women	• Reduces anaemia in girls – often more severe than in boys. Lack of iron adversely influences school attendance and achievement. • Reduces gender disparity.
MDG # 4 Reduce child mortality	• Reduces serious consequences on child health, including low birth weight and stillbirth. • Reduces child mortality.
MDG # 5 Improve maternal health	• Reduces maternal anaemia. • Reduces the maternal mortality ratio (20% of maternal deaths are directly attributed to anaemia)

Source: Cavalli-Sforza T, *et al.* Weekly iron folic acid supplementation of women of reproductive age: impact overview, lessons learned, expansion plans, and contributions toward achievement of the Millennium Development Goals. *Nutrition reviews*, December 2005; 63(12): S152-S158.

With a policy of WIFS for WRA in place, programme interventions are legitimized and this facilitates implementation. Establishing policies is essential for commitment to the programme and also for resource allocation, which helps in overcoming important political, programme, social and structural barriers. These issues are well reflected in the evolution of WIFS programmes in India and Egypt. In India, the recommendations of the National Consultation on Anaemia Control, held in 1997,[4] stated:

> 'Adolescent girls on attaining menarche should consume one IFA tablet containing 100mg elemental iron and 500 mcg Folic acid once a week. This should be accompanied by appropriate dietary counselling. Considering the large size of the adolescent population, as well as the financial and operational constraints, it is recommended that district-level pilot projects should be undertaken. The total duration of a weekly dose of iron supplements, its cost-effectiveness and operational feasibility should be examined.'

This recommendation was followed by a launch of district- and state-level demonstration projects in many parts of India and finally in the inclusion of WIFS to adolescent girls in the State Implementation Plans of selected states under the National Rural Health Mission (NRHM). Experience reveals that policy formulation, combined with a high-profile programme launch, facilitates in gaining political support during the implementation phase.

---

4   National Consultation on Control of Nutritional Anaemia in India, Nirman Bhavan, New Delhi, 16-17 October 1997, Ministry of Health and Family Welfare.

4. Target population and strategy for accessing IFA supplements

> Anaemia programmes for WRA in developing countries include targeting adolescent girls both in and out of school, as well as WRA who are in communities or are part of the workforce. WIFS programmes ideally need to target WRA across all socioeconomic groups, since anaemia prevalence is high in this population group irrespective of the economic conditions. In order for all WRA to have access to WIFS, a strategy of providing free WIFS for economically disadvantaged WRA needs to be combined with promoting the purchase of WIFS at a reasonable price for women with a higher socioeconomic status, using a social-marketing approach.

Distinct strategies should be used in designing WIFS programmes for four primary sections of the WRA population: adolescent girls in schools, adolescent girls out of school, women in factories or other workplaces or institutions, and women in communities. Non-pregnant WRA are a section of the population that is not routinely reached through the health sector. Involvement of non-health sectors and establishing links with various ongoing development programmes, as well as building on institutional or non-formal networks of WRA, is effective in reaching these women. Effective strategies for contacting and working with WRA in WIFS programmes include reaching adolescent girls in schools, using a school-to-community approach, and selecting and training community volunteers, women union leaders, teachers and front-line workers of health and other development programmes dealing with WRA.

It is estimated that almost one third of adolescent girls in developing countries are married and conceive within a year of marriage[5]. Within the WRA group, designing and implementing WIFS programmes for adolescent girls has therefore been accorded a high priority because of the need to build pre-pregnancy iron stores and prevent the serious complications of ID during pregnancy. Moreover, reaching this section of the WRA population is a good start in addressing anaemia in WRA, since females at this age are more responsive and motivated to take action when mobilized in school or community groups. Additionally, it is envisaged

---

5   *National Family Health Survey (NFHS-3),* 2005-06, Volume II. Mumbai, International Institute for Population Sciences.

that establishing a habit of regularly consuming WIFS in adolescence will help build a habit of consuming IFA supplements in adulthood and will also improve compliance during pregnancy.

The senior-school education sector, with or without involvement of the health sector, has been clearly shown to be the most effective channel for reaching adolescent girls in school in all four WIFS programmes in India and in other countries such as Cambodia, Egypt and the Lao People's Democratic Republic. Experiences from developing countries demonstrate that the success of scaled-up programmes is also due to schoolgirls reaching out to disadvantaged girls who are not in school in a "girl-to-girl" or "girl-to-community" approach. This dimension of WIFS programmes for adolescent girls in schools adds further value to school-based WIFS programmes. A successfully implemented girl-to-girl approach involves forming a club or core group of 15-20 schoolgirls who are trained to be "nodal girls". Each nodal girl is assigned the responsibility of reaching a minimum of one to three adolescent girls who are not in school. The responsibility of regularly supplying IFA supplements, counselling on the benefits of regular weekly use of supplements, managing any side-effects reported and monitoring consumption by out-of-school girls have all been successfully carried out by schoolgirls who are trained and assigned those tasks. In fact, the Uttar Pradesh WIFS Programme clearly indicates that girls assigned such responsibilities take pride in their tasks and are motivated by the fact that schoolteachers and the community recognize their contributions and view them as having special leadership qualities.

The components and strategies used in a WIFS programme are governed by the central decision on whether IFA supplements will be provided free of cost to WRA. Consumption of WIFS is expected to continue throughout the reproductive life cycle, until other ways of ensuring adequate iron and folic acid status in the population are achieved through dietary improvement. The policy of free distribution of WIFS to WRA is therefore an effective short-term strategy and has been the policy choice of developing countries, such as Cambodia, Egypt, India and Viet Nam, that have scaled up their programmes. As reported by the WIFS programme in Yen Bai Province in Viet Nam, provision of free IFA ensures equitable distribution and higher participation of poorer, more disadvantaged women, especially ethnic minorities. Since ID and anaemia in WRA is prevalent across socioeconomic situations, a two-pronged strategy is needed, comprising free distribution of supplements to a defined low socioeconomic population and social marketing of the supplements at a reasonable cost to those WRA who can afford them. This, along with measures to promote the consumption of foods rich in iron, would provide a sustainable solution to improve iron status.

5. Composition, presentation and supply of IFA supplements

> Documented programme experiences demonstrate that the specifications of IFA supplements with reference to: composition, colour (red), size, shape (round or elliptical), coating of tablets, presentation details (such as packaging, nomenclature, attractiveness of illustration or labelling and information printed on benefits) and having a designated "WIFS Day/Iron Day" contribute significantly to the success of a WRA programme. Attractive blister packaging (4, 5 or 10 tablets per blister) enhances the value of the product. In the absence of availability of a distinct packaged product for weekly consumption by WRA, IFA tablets used daily during pregnancy could be successfully used for weekly consumption by WRA. For a WIFS programme to be successful, it is essential that an uninterrupted supply of good quality IFA supplements, at a low cost, is ensured through partnership with the private sector.

The 10 WIFS programmes reviewed indicate two levels of elemental iron in the IFA supplement used—60mg and 100mg—in the form of ferrous sulphate. The folic acid content of the supplements used varied widely— from 0.3mg to 3.5mg. It is evident from the case studies that in situations where no special supplements are produced for WRA, IFA supplements designed for daily use during pregnancy can be successfully used as a weekly supplement for non-pregnant WRA. However, based on the research findings reviewed at the WHO Global Consultation on Weekly Iron and Folic Acid Supplementation for Preventing Anaemia in Women of Reproductive Age, held in Manila, Philippines, in 2007, IFA tablets for once-a-week consumption by WRA are recommended to contain a minimum of 60mg of elemental iron and a much higher level of folic acid of 2.8 mg per tablet. The increase is recommended to build proper folic acid storage at the pre-pregnancy stage to prevent neurotubular defects in newborn infants. Although, for effective programme management, it is desirable to promote the use of an IFA supplement that is specifically designed and produced for WRA, the programmes in India demonstrate that logistical management of IFA supplements, even when identical to the supply used for pregnant mothers, is feasible as well as safe and effective for non-pregnant women.

It is evident from the analysis of programme experiences that the colour and shape of IFA tablets are important factors in promoting their consumption. Red or pink IFA tablets are reportedly well accepted and are often associated with "strengthening the blood". Coating tablets with colour film also helps to their increase stability and shelf life in different storage conditions and reduces the side-effects of nausea and vomiting, which are caused by gastric irritation. Sugar-coating tablets improves their taste but should not be encouraged since it increases the chances of the IFA tablets being mistaken for sweets and swallowed by children, with grave and in some cases fatal consequences (depending on the age of the child and number of tablets ingested). Small, elliptical tablets are reported to be well accepted and easy to swallow. Moreover, tablets with a distinct design and colour are beneficial so that they are not mistaken for contraceptives or sweets.

The experiences of various countries indicate that packaging IFA tablets attractively, not only increases the value of the product, but also contributes to a positive image and helps sustain interest and demand. Moreover, appropriate packaging contributes to ease of storage and monitoring. The number of tablets to be packaged in one pack or blister strip depends on what users can afford and the frequency of contact the delivery system has with WRA. It has been demonstrated that blister packs containing at least one month's supply of four tablets in a strip is practical for public health service providers and for marketing purposes. A blister pack of four or 10 WIFS tablets was reported to be acceptable to WRA who purchased WIFS in Cambodia, the Philippines and Hai Duong Province in Viet Nam. In the WIFS programme in Yen Bai Province in Viet Nam, however, blister packs were designed as tear off strips of five tablets, which was practical for free distribution. In all the four India-based WIFS programmes, tablets were supplied free of cost in lots of four to five tablets or 10 tablets. The WIFS blisters of 4-10 tablets were cut out from the blister-pack sheets of 30 tablets that were used for supplying a minimum of 90 IFA supplement tablets during the three antenatal visits with pregnant mothers. This system is practical, since no special tablets need to be produced or packed for the weekly supplies for non-pregnant women and adolescent girls.

It is evident that each country needs to review and agree on the form and composition of supplements for its WIFS programme. In cases where IFA supplements are provided free of cost by the Government or another channel, the number of tablets to be included in each blister pack will be governed by the frequency of contact between providers and recipients, as well as the convenience of monitoring supply and consumption. In cases where WIFS are purchased, a market study should be carried out to determine the optimum number of tablets and the price that WRA are willing and able to pay for them, both in the short term and over several years.

The quality and attractiveness of packaging add to the cost of IFA supplements. In India, the cost to the Government of purchasing a mass supply of IFA supplements was only about US$0.12 for a one-year supply of 52 IFA tablets, with each tablet containing 100 mg of elemental iron and 0.5 mg of folic acid. In the Philippines, WIFS supplements were not supplied free of cost, but were sold in pharmacies at a much higher price of about US$0.14 for just one tablet. The supplements had a much higher folic acid content (3.5mg) and a lower iron content (60mg) than the Indian supplements. Moreover, they were produced and supplied by a private pharmaceutical agency in attractive, colourful packs, with the objective of creating market demand.

In situations where WRA are part of a government-managed public health programme, the packaging cost needs to be reduced to a minimum. In cases where the central strategy is for WRA to purchase WIFS, supply and packaging design should be such that supplements are easily affordable but still attractive enough to enhance compliance. The case studies demonstrate that it is very useful to have information regarding the best time to take the tablets, the benefits of WIFS and the designated WIFS day printed on cartons or packages of IFA supplements. A product name and positive illustration on packs also increases acceptance, demand and purchase. A distinct attractive logo, highlighting the association of IFA supplements with health and beauty, further increases the value of the supplement for WRA and helps to achieve a shift from viewing WIFS as a medicine to a long-term strategy for protection of health and beauty.

An external quality monitoring mechanism is useful and needs to be put in place for periodic checking of the quality of IFA supplements. Establishing such a system will ensure that the approved standards of composition and quality are maintained. Additionally, countries should aim to develop the capacity of local pharmaceutical companies to produce supplements of accepted quality, with the right composition and appropriate packaging and cost.

6. Procurement and delivery of IFA supplements

> It is critical to ensure the availability of resources and the appropriate management of supplies, including correctly estimating requirements, so that there is an adequate supply of IFA supplements for the WIFS programme. Supply channels, based on the country's agreed strategy, need to be clearly defined so that supply is streamlined. Also, as IFA supplements need to be made available and accessible to WRA of various ages, in a wide range of situations, dependency on a single delivery system is not advisable. Dovetailing WIFS programmes with other available infrastructures and networks, particularly the education sector, is feasible, sustainable and low-cost. Marketing supplements using social-marketing strategies is effective when WIFS are readily available for purchase at an affordable price through various community groups, NGOs and other institutional set-ups.

Establishing a mechanism for streamlining an uninterrupted supply of IFA tablets, whether they are distributed free of cost or through a social-marketing strategy, is critical for ensuring a regular supply on a long-term basis. Supply of WIFS to nodal government departments, if the Government is in partnership with the private system, improves the sustainability of WIFS programmes. Pilot testing and establishing a suitable supply system is essential prior to scaling up a WIFS programme.

The annual supply requirement for WRA can be estimated by multiplying 52 tablets/person/year by the estimated number of WRA recipients projected to be reached, with an additional 20% for buffer stock. Taking into consideration the resources and storage facilities available, the entire annual supply of IFA could be procured at one time to reduce cost, since IFA supplements have a good shelf life. Channels for supply of IFA supplements, from production to procurement to service providers to consumers, will depend entirely on whether the IFA tablets are distributed free of charge or marketed to WRA. Allocating resources and defining the roles and responsibilities of government sectors, the private pharmaceutical industry and donors will ensure an adequate and consistent supply. An external system could be established by the government, in partnership with private industry, if required, for periodic checking of the quality and logistical management of IFA supplements.

It is evident from the experiences of the WIFS programmes in various countries that it is not practical or cost-effective to be dependent on a single delivery channel, such as health, to optimize coverage of the target population. Dovetailing WIFS programmes with other available infrastructures and networks is feasible, sustainable and cost-effective. Adolescent girls in schools are easily reached by establishing a link with the middle- and secondary-school system. Teachers can be well accepted by schoolgirls as distributors and monitors of IFA supplements. For example, during the one-month Ramadan period in Egypt, the WIFS programme demonstrated that the supplements continued to be used at home by students provided the school ensured the required supply of WIFS and teachers directed students to consume IFA supplements one to two hours after breaking their fast with a meal.

In situations where free supply of WIFS to WRA is implemented as a part of the public health programme, teachers, female leaders and leaders of religious institutions have been accepted by the community as credible and effective distributors. It has been estimated in the WIFS programme in Egypt that tablet distribution by a teacher to about 45 students in a class requires about 10-15 minutes. For effective distribution of WIFS, it is crucial that the location and frequency of distribution is specified and widely disseminated to WRA and the community. It is also crucial to ensure the availability of drinking water at distribution points in institutional or community set-ups.

In situations where WRA can afford to buy IFA supplements, social marketing has been used successfully as a strategy for reaching non-pregnant WRA. In Cambodia, for example, responses to buying IFA supplements were better in higher socioeconomic groups compared with lower ones. A social-marketing strategy is of particular significance for non-pregnant, non-adolescent women of higher socioeconomic groups who are also anaemic but are not reached by the public health system. Moreover, purchase of WIFS through a social-marketing approach rather than free supply is a sustainable solution, since WRA need to consume WIFS throughout

> Purchase of WIFS through a social-marketing approach rather than free supply can be a sustainable solution, since WRA need to consume WIFS throughout their entire reproductive lives, unless iron-rich food or iron/folic acid-fortified food is readily available to the population.

their entire reproductive lives, unless iron-rich food or iron/folic acid-fortified food is readily available to the population.

The planning and implementation of an effective social-marketing programme has demonstrated positive results in terms of demand creation, sustaining satisfactory sales and high compliance. A successful social-marketing strategy requires a quality IFA supplement product being available at the correct price and place. Ensuring the availability of and access to IFA supplements at an affordable price in traditional drug stores and local village or urban shops encourages WRA to buy the supplements as over-the-counter products. Additionally, IFA supplements can be made readily available and accessible through various groups, including: NGOs, networks of community volunteers, community development programmes, self-help groups, micro-credit groups of women, marriage registration systems, centres for family planning, centres for family welfare, centres for women's development, and youth programmes, as well as through networking with organized and non-organized WRA groups employed in factories and other workplaces.

The role of private partnership with the pharmaceutical sector is of special significance since it has demonstrably contributed, not only to ensuring a regular supply of supplements, but also to promoting regular use of WIFS through appropriate marketing strategies based on the findings of community-specific market research. However, as indicated by the Philippines' WIFS programme, it is essential that government policy on WIFS for WRA contains a statement on the role of the private sector in preventing anaemia in order to sustain the interest and long-term involvement of the private pharmaceutical industry.

7. Communication strategy to create demand and improve coverage and compliance

> Complementing the regular supply of IFA supplements with an effective communication strategy is a critical factor in the success of WIFS programmes, and formative research is useful for the development of such strategies. Sharing the benefits of WIFS experienced by WRA in peer-group discussions has been demonstrated to be a very effective communication strategy, while dissemination of information on the day designated as "WIFS Day" and promoting consumption of WIFS on this day facilitates increased compliance. A social-marketing approach, while it can be expensive, has long-term benefits and could be used in WIFS programmes to motivate target groups and influence the adoption of positive purchasing and consumption behaviour. Social-mobilization actions, such as high-profile launches, mass media broadcasts and community-based activities like rallies, debates, folk songs, etc. are critical in creating a supportive community environment.

One of the most important components of a WIFS programme is the communication strategy, which should have the following three main objectives:

1. To grant high priority to the WIFS programme.
2. To create demand for iron-folic acid tablets.
3. To motivate the target population to regularly consume the supplements.

In developing an effective communication strategy, including social mobilization and social marketing, an essential first step is to conduct formative research on the current knowledge, attitudes and practices related to iron and folic acid deficiency, anaemia and its prevention. Such research needs to be conducted among all WRA, including: adolescent girls both in and out of school, non-adolescent and newly married women, pregnant and lactating women, influential members of the community, youth and female leaders and university students. Additionally, it is advantageous to include other stakeholders in the study, such as policy-makers, programme managers, providers of health services and education, women's development institutions, women's workplace and community leaders, and pharmaceutical managers.

The research should aim to seek information regarding:

- dietary practices and sources of iron-folic acid consumption;
- facilitating factors and barriers to acquiring IFA supplements for WRA;
- attitudes and practices related to regularly purchasing and taking IFA tablets;
- issues related to the supply of IFA supplements;
- views on optimal presentation of the product in terms of colour, shape, packaging, and price;
- viable channels for distribution or purchase of IFA tablets; and
- acceptability of WIFS by front-line workers in the health and non-health sectors.

WIFS programmes in Cambodia, Egypt, the Lao People's Democratic Republic, the Philippines and Hai Duong Province in Viet Nam have demonstrated that comprehensive formative research can provide useful insights for appropriate positioning of the product, communication messages, logo design and standardization of the information to be printed on IFA packages. Moreover, research findings can also assist in the formulation of communication strategies, including the use of specific communication channels, such as: interpersonal communications, multiple communication channels, mass media (TV and radio) and local community-based programmes (skits and health fairs, etc). The communication campaign and related support materials, as well as tools for counselling and for creating a supportive environment, should be based, as far as possible, on the results of formative research. Findings from the WIFS programme in Egypt also revealed that formative research can be useful in identifying innovative methods to motivate students and caregivers.

An analysis of the case studies revealed that IFA supplements should be positioned, not as a medicine to cure anaemia, but as a positive intervention, along with dietary measures, to improve iron status, prevent IDA and enhance the overall quality of life.

An analysis of the case studies revealed that IFA supplements should be positioned, not as a medicine to cure anaemia, but as a positive intervention, along with dietary measures, to improve iron status, prevent IDA and enhance the overall quality of life. The WIFS programme in the Philippines revealed that, in order to translate awareness of the significance of WIFS into the practice of regularly purchasing and consuming IFA supplements, it is vital that communication strategies encourage WRA to perceive WIFS as a measure for improving health and appearance, rather than as a therapeutic product. However, communication efforts still need to educate the community regarding common symptoms, such as dizziness, fatigue and paleness, which are often due to ID and can be prevented through the regular use of WIFS.

The focus of the communication action plan should be to sensitize all stakeholders at various levels – from health and education planners to service providers of WIFS—regarding the wide range of benefits of WIFS. A comprehensive communication strategy should:

- address the relevant target groups;
- impact policy-makers to encourage them to invest in WIFS programmes; and
- ensure a shift in the attitudes and behaviour of WRA that results in regular purchasing and consumption of WIFS.

In Egypt, the communication strategy targeted students and the community message stressed the role of WIFS in terms of mental development, school performance, energy and physical growth. This was reported as being acceptable and convincing. In WIFS programmes where adolescent girls in schools are the target, the following three-tiered communication actions are reported to be effective: school-level activities, reinforcement of messages at the home level and mobilization of community support.

To promote routine consumption of WIFS and sustain a high level of compliance, it is critical that recipients, and the community, are informed of the benefits of WIFS. The benefits often reported to influence behaviour are those that are readily experienced by WRA following consumption of WIFS. These include improved concentration in school, feeling stronger and less tired, increased energy levels and output in day-to-day work, increased appetite, improved overall capacity to work and earn, better sleep, improved skin appearance, regularization of menstruation, and building of pre-pregnancy health. Communication strategies must encourage sharing of these benefits, through community and peer-group interactions, in order to create a supportive environment for the WIFS programme and to increase demand and compliance. Such a strategy was demonstrated to be effective in the Bihar and Madhya Pradesh WIFS programmes in India.

Recipients should also be informed of side-effects, such as black stools, nausea and vomiting, but care should be taken to present the information on adverse side-effects in such a manner that there is less significance attached to these than to the benefits. The tendency to overemphasize side-effects should be discouraged for the following two well-documented reasons: the reported adverse effects are often transitory and the frequency of WIFS side-effects is much lower than with daily doses. Moreover, side-effects decrease over time, as reported by the programmes in Egypt and the Lao People's Democratic Republic.

Advice to WRA to consume WIFS on a full stomach, at least two hours after dinner, prior to retiring at night, reduces the incidence of side-effects and improves iron absorption. This advice should be part of the communication strategy, as was the case in three India programmes (Uttar Pradesh, Gujarat, Madhya Pradesh) and in the Lao People's Democratic Republic. Such measures have been shown to increase compliance. A compliance survey conducted early in the implementation phase is beneficial in modifying plans and introducing measures to sustain high compliance. Viet Nam's programmes demonstrated that WRA, if convinced at the start of the project through an effective communication strategy, maintain high compliance. It has been well documented by various programmes that high compliance of WIFS can be achieved, irrespective of supervision, provided recipients are convinced of the benefits of WIFS through an effective communication strategy and a system is in place for monitoring consumption.

Including female front-line workers in programmes as beneficiaries of WIFS has been demonstrated to be a useful social-mobilization strategy. Additionally, community-based actions, such as organizing periodic sessions and conducting campaigns to motivate people to buy or use WIFS, are critical in generating a supportive environment. In special situations, such as harvesting season, modifications need to be introduced into the communication strategy, as was done in the programme in Hai Duong Province in Viet Nam, to sustain demand for WIFS and remind busy women to consume IFA supplements every week.

An active effort needs to be made to be vigilant and take timely actions to discourage the spread of any incorrect rumours that may be detrimental to the operation of the WIFS programme. In the programme in Hai Duong Province in Viet Nam, activities were implemented regularly to counteract any negative influences. In Cambodia, rumours that the IFA tablets contained amphetamine to make women work harder and also had a contraceptive effect were handled by addressing these issues through a well-planned communication strategy.

Communication strategies are distinctly different for WIFS programmes where supplements are not supplied free of charge. If WRA are to be mobilized to purchase WIFS, an effective social-marketing and social-mobilization programme is required. Such a programme needs to be positioned around the 4 Ps of marketing:

- Product (importance and benefits);
- Price (information on cost and encouragement to buy IFA tablets) ;
- Place (availability of IFA tablets at all times); and
- Promotion (of the product, price and place including advertising, packaging, point of sale displays and special events).

Experiences of social-marketing strategies in Cambodia, the Lao People's Democratic Republic and the Philippines, and in Hai Duong Province in Viet Nam, indicate that the positive positioning of IFA supplements is very effective.

Demand creation through an attractively presented product that appeals to WRA is of prime importance. Additionally, a distinct name and image, promoted through a well-planned communication strategy, increases the acceptance of WIFS. A logo for the product designed around the concept of iron supplements and their impact on health and beauty, is well accepted when complemented by a standardized "catchy" message. Logos used in various programmes have included a picture of an attractive "blossoming young woman" or of a beautiful girl holding a rose. To promote the product and reinforce the message, logos and standardized messages may also be printed on varied materials, such as fliers, billboards, banners etc. In Cambodia's programme, sharing of information on haemoglobin levels was noted to be a factor in motivating secondary-school girls to purchase IFA supplements.

To create demand, communication and social-marketing strategies need to be complemented by well-planned social-mobilization activities. Experiences reveal that involvement of the community is critical to creating an appropriately supportive environment and for the success and sustainability of WIFS programmes, while mobilization of local leaders is important for successful implementation. The WIFS programme in the Lao People's Democratic Republic indicated that organizing field visits to project sites is useful in generating the interest and support of political leaders. Social-mobilization activities there proved effective in securing leadership support from community members as well as influential members of the community, administrators and politicians. A high-profile programme launch, with involvement of senior administrators and politicians, adds further value to social-mobilization efforts. In addition, social-mobilization campaigns focusing on women adopting WIFS as a regular habit act as reminders and motivate community members or busy women to purchase and consume tablets. Such promotional reinforcement activities are also important in counteracting any negative influences and trends, such as incorrect information or rumours relating to the routine consumption of supplements.

A fixed-day approach for distribution and consumption of WIFS can be promoted through the communication strategy. This concept was used with great success across all 10 WIFS programmes reviewed. A fixed-day approach has been observed, not only to serve as a good reminder to WRA and the community to consume WIFS, but also to be a very effective programme management tool. To select a designated WIFS Day, the local situation needs to be taken into consideration. Use of a fixed day for consumption of WIFS addresses the issue of forgetfulness, which has been identified as the major factor adversely influencing compliance. Placing an IFA tablet on a pillow on the fixed day acts as an effective reminder and should be promoted.

> A fixed-day approach, not only serves as a good reminder to WRA and the community to consume WIFS, but is also a very effective programme-management tool.

8. Capacity development

> For capacity development, training plans and content need to be formulated based on the identified roles and responsibilities of the various stakeholders in the WIFS programme. Technical information on WIFS should be accurate and standardized. Training should stress, not only technical details, but also skills in the management of supply logistics, use of IEC materials and monitoring. For adolescents, training in family-life education, rather than merely in prevention measures for ID and anaemia, is important in sustaining the interest of trainees. The training plan also needs to ensure the building of capacity of at least one selected institution to undertake laboratory testing to respond to any WIFS programme requirements.

Ensuring uniform understanding is critical to effective coordination of the health and non-health sectors. It is therefore crucial to define the roles and responsibilities of stakeholders and to identify the knowledge as well as the skills required for effective execution of those responsibilities. Table 3 presents an example of stakeholders and their responsibilities. Development of a training package or training manual is important to facilitate the standardization of information imparted at various levels, including the pharmaceutical and advertising sectors, and to ensure that training provides accurate and relevant information to perform the assigned tasks.

Training content should focus on the importance of preventing ID and anaemia; the benefits of preventing ID; measures for the prevention of ID, including dietary sources of iron; and the significance of WIFS. Additionally, training should put special effort into imparting skills in conducting group and interpersonal counselling, including the use of communication aids. Equally important is training on IFA supply logistics, management of IFA sales and consumption, completion of monitoring forms and analysis of information at the local level, and monitoring of sales and usage of supplements, as well skills in management of funds.

	Table 3: Development of training plans – defining stakeholders and their responsibilities	
I	At government level	Stakeholders - Ministry of Health and Family Welfare; Departments of Health, Nutrition, Secondary Education, Women's Development, Rural and Urban Development; managers of private-sector organizations Responsibilities – Formulate and implement WIFS strategies and policy. Establish a monitoring mechanism. Allocate resources —financial, human and organizational.
II	Nodal professional bodies (public health- or nutrition-related) and research institutes	Responsibilities • Advocacy for according high priority to anaemia prevention and control in WRA. • Technical support in formulation of policy and strategy, education and training of trainers, training of nodal service providers. • Participation in formative research, monitoring and evaluation. • Provision of support for timely action to resolve constraints.
III	Health programme manager	Responsibilities • Training and supervision of staff for effective implementation of plan, using a fixed-day approach for distribution to recipients. • Ensuring timely and regular procurement of supplies and logistics management. • Creation of demand for WIFS and ensuring high compliance. • Monitoring of implementation, including social mobilization and education activities • Periodic checking of compliance through group discussions, etc. • Management of resources.
IV	Education programme manager	Responsibilities • Ensuring the fixed-day strategy is put into operation in schools for adolescent girls. • Establishment of systems for assessment of WIFS supply. Logistics management. • Monitoring of reports on usage and compliance, shared regularly with health department. • Communication strategy on prevention of anaemia through diet and supplements. High compliance of WIFS. • Maintaining ability to undertake family-life education sessions.

	Table 3: Development of training plans – defining stakeholders and their responsibilities	
V	Health care providers / teachers / community leaders.	Responsibilities • Distribution of IFA supplements. • Effective counselling of WRA to influence behaviour as regards dietary modifications and regular WIFS consumption. • Ensuring teachers and health workers are equipped to undertake family-life education sessions. • Identification of constraints and taking of timely actions to resolve compliance problems. • Monitoring of WIFS supply and consumption.
VI	Adolescent girls in school / out of school and other WRA	Responsibilities • Awareness of the significance of anaemia and its prevention. • Obtaining IFA supplements regularly — institutionalizing a fixed-day system to facilitate regular consumption. • Consuming supplements regularly and managing side-effects. • Reporting constraints to health care providers / teachers — side-effects or inaccessibility of supply.

In the case of adolescent girls, training in how to improve iron status and prevent anaemia could be positioned as a part of family-life education. Such a comprehensive training approach is much more acceptable to adolescent girls who are at a stage of life where they are curious about a number of issues related to physical changes in their bodies and are also interested in building their self image and understanding their social environment. Skills in counselling their peer groups should also be a part of the training. The training content could be modified for trainers, including teachers. To encourage question/answer sessions, use of a "question box" has proved effective, since such a system gives an opportunity to young girls, who are often very shy, to raise questions without revealing their identities.

The training plans must include ensuring the capacity of selected institutions to conduct laboratory tests, such as haemoglobin and serum ferritin estimations.

9. Monitoring

Monitoring of WIFS programmes is critical to effective implementation and high compliance. Simple, standardized individual and group registers for recording supply and compliance have proved effective for monitoring supply, usage and compliance. Individual monitoring cards, maintained by consumers, are also effective tools for reinforcing messages and act as reminders for consumption of WIFS. In the case of programmes based on social marketing of WIFS, recording sales figures is a useful tool for monitoring supply and usage.

Monitoring details should ideally be included in the planning stage of the WIFS programme. A standardized, user-friendly monitoring format, designed to help enter data on supply, distribution and consumption of IFA supplements in minimum time, is critical. All four Indian programmes have demonstrated the positive impact monitoring can have on WIFS programmes by improving coverage, reducing drop-outs and increasing WIFS compliance. Monitoring forms in the Gujarat and Bihar programmes are simple, with one red circle against the fixed WIFS day of each week or simply a cluster of four red circles per month. The format focuses on individual monitoring by WRA and entering of information on a monthly basis in a central register.

A number of studies have demonstrated that, in school-based WIFS programmes, individual cards held by WRA are useful. During scaling-up, such a monitoring system may be difficult to sustain. However, individual monitoring or compliance cards have proved to be a very effective tool for reinforcing messages on the benefits of regular usage of WIFS and for acting as a reminder to consume WIFS on WIFS Day. Use of such a format therefore plays a significant role in improving compliance, since in three WIFS programmes (Uttar Pradesh and Gujarat in India and the Lao People's Democratic Republic), forgetfulness was reported to be the primary reason for reductions in compliance.

Use of monitoring registers at a class or school level, with information entered each week by each adolescent girl, has also been reported to be practical, simple and acceptable to teachers. In such registers, specific columns are used for recording information on side-effects and reasons for discontinuation of WIFS. The information is very useful in following up cases of low compliance and organizing counselling sessions. Similar monitoring registers are recommended for other institutional set-ups, such as factories or other workplaces. In situations where the implementation strategy has been dovetailed with ongoing programmes for WRA, monitoring information related to WIFS could be linked with existing monitoring systems. The WIFS programme in Egypt indicated that development and use of software for rapid compilation of WIFS monitoring data at the district level can be useful and facilitates problem-solving. In countries where WIFS are promoted for purchase by WRA, pharmaceutical retailers can play an important role in monitoring supply and consumption.

Mechanisms need to be established for review of emerging data in periodic monitoring-committee meetings, with the participation of various stakeholders. In a school situation, formation of a school WIFS committee, with teacher and student representation, has been found to facilitate regular monitoring and appropriate management of the programme. Such a forum helps facilitate regular review and timely action for revisiting intervention strategies and the operational plan. Monitoring mechanisms need to be further strengthened by the inclusion of outcome and impact indicators for the WIFS programme in surveys organized routinely at either the national or regional level.

10. Evaluation

> Evaluation should review the effectiveness and constraints of a wide range of WIFS programme components including policy, training, IEC, supply of supplements, system of compliance, assessment, monitoring and cost. Both process and impact indicators should be a part of the evaluation design. Key indicators should be selected based on the local programme situation. The WHO Global Consultation on Weekly Iron and Folic Acid Supplementation for Preventing Anaemia in Women of Reproductive Age recommended annual evaluation for the first five years, with close monitoring considered desirable in the first year.

Evaluation, including process and impact evaluation, should be integrated into the WIFS programme plan from the start of the programme. Process evaluation provides information to review the effectiveness and constraints of a strategy, while impact evaluation helps determine if the programme is having the desired impact on haemoglobin levels, anaemia prevalence, iron and folate status and other biological parameters. The laboratory methods used should be standardized. Since the WIFS programme, to a great extent, is dependent upon the achievement of behavioural aims and objectives, it is crucial that the evaluation design includes assessment of the knowledge, attitudes and practices of programme agents and beneficiaries, compliance in taking the supplements and cost per recipient. Annual evaluation for the first five years was recommended by the WHO Global Consultation on Weekly Iron and Folic Acid Supplementation for Preventing Anaemia in Women of Reproductive Age, (Manila, Philippines, 25-27 April 2007), while close monitoring was considered desirable in the first year. Evaluation conducted early in the implementation phase is beneficial for modification of plans and for making timely strategic shifts in programme implementation. WIFS programme managers, based on programme requirements, can decide which indicators are feasible and desirable.

A successful WIFS programme can reduce anaemia while improving maternal health, fetal health, child survival, work productivity and school performance. In 2008-2009, WHO undertook a review of 10 WIFS programmes in six countries. Several common themes underpinning the success of those programmes emerged and are summarized below.

More information is contained within the document Weekly iron and folic acid supplementation programmes for women of reproductive age: an analysis of best programme practices (full version), Manila, World Health Organization Regional Office for the Western Pacific, 2011. See also the WHO WPRO website: http://www.wpro.who.int/health_topics/nutrition/publications.htm.

BEST PRACTICE TOP 10

1	Building iron nutrition prior to pregnancy is critical. Therefore, an anaemia control programme needs to **address both pregnant and non-pregnant women** of reproductive age (WRA), including adolescent girls (10-19 years).
2	**Policy-makers need to be made aware** of the severity and prevalence of ID and anaemia and the simple and cost-effective way it can be addressed through the implementation of a Weekly Iron and Folic Acid Supplementation (WIFS) programme.
3	Anaemia affects WRA irrespective of socioeconomic status. Thus, **WIFS need to be made accessible to all WRA** by: - providing **free supplements** for economically disadvantaged women, and - **selling supplements** at an affordable price to those who have a higher socioeconomic status.
4	**Creating a partnership** between government sectors (Ministries of Health) and the private sector (pharmaceutical companies) helps to ensure a regular and low-cost IFA supply and enhances overall programme sustainability.

BEST PRACTICE TOP 10

5
Using schools as the primary vehicle for reaching adolescent girls with WIFS is extremely effective.

Training schoolgirls to reach other girls who are not in school and provide them with access to IFA supplements can be a very successful strategy.

6
WIFS presentation matters. Having attractive packaging and an eye-catching logo or slogan is important.

7
Supervision of consumption is not required, but **simple monitoring formats**, such as **individual monitoring cards or group registers, are effective in providing the necessary information** for the smooth running of the WIFS programme and for encouraging compliance.

8
Appearance matters. The size, shape and colour of IFA supplements are important.

9
Good communication is key

Creating the public perception that WIFS are preventive guardians of health and beauty rather than medicine is important for increasing individual compliance.

Encouraging community discussion about the benefits of taking WIFS is important for improving women's attitudes towards the intervention and increasing compliance.

10
Selecting a fixed day in the week to be **WIFS Day** effectively addresses the problem of "forgetfulness" in programme participants and thus **improves compliance.**